Learn About Books

Strange Animals

Written by
Bobbie Whitcombe

BRIMAX BOOKS • NEWMARKET • ENGLAND

There are many different kinds of animal in the world. Some look very strange to us. Others have some surprising habits.

Look at this strange lizard. The **thorny devil** lives in the deserts of Australia. Its scales are long and spiky. On cold nights, dew forms on them and provides the creature with a drink!

The **giant anteater** has a long snout like a tube. It has no teeth, but it can lick up ants and termites with its long sticky tongue.

The **flamingo** has
a very long neck
and long legs.
It needs a long neck
to reach down into
the water and mud.
It feeds with its head
upside down!

Is this a bird or a mammal? The
duck-billed platypus has a beak and
webbed feet like a duck, but the furry
body of a mammal. It uses its webbed
feet for swimming. But it has claws
to dig its nest. In fact, it is one of
the few mammals that lays eggs.

Animals have some interesting ways of keeping themselves safe from enemies.

The skin of the **armadillo** is covered in scaly, bony plates. They are like a knight's suit of armour, which is how the armadillo got its name.

Opossums pretend to be dead when they are in danger. This one is lying very still until the bobcat goes away.

The **frilled lizard** has a wide fold of skin around its neck. When there is danger, the frill stands up and makes it look fierce. It also opens its mouth wide and hisses to scare its attackers.

The **porcupine** uses its sharp quills as a weapon. If an enemy threatens it, the porcupine charges backwards. It stabs the quills into the animal's face.

The **sea slug** floats
on the surface of the
water. It feeds on
jellyfish. It stores
the poison from the
jellyfish's long
stinging tentacles in
its own body. Then the
slug can use the
poison if it is
attacked.

The South American **electric eel** uses
electricity to defend itself. It can
kill other fish by giving them an electric
shock which would be strong enough to
knock a man over.

Some animals use their bright skin colours to warn off enemies.

The **fire salamander** has bright markings to warn any predators that it is poisonous and dangerous to eat.

The bright colours of the **arrow-poison frog** are a warning of its deadly poison.

The pattern on the back of this **giant peacock moth's** wings looks like a pair of eyes. Birds think it is a much bigger creature than it really is.

Some animals use disguise to avoid being seen by others.

The **spider crab** has a spiny body which collects weed on it as it moves along. This helps it to hide on the sea shore as it waits to dart out at its prey.

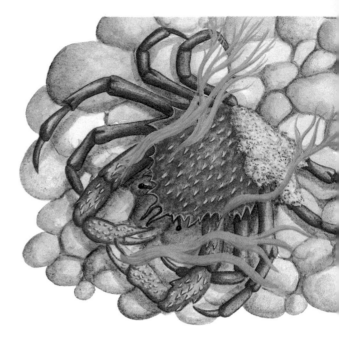

Look at this **leaf fish** standing on its head. It looks like a leaf to any big fish that is passing.

Can you see the
creature on this plant?
It is a **stick insect**.
It moves very slowly
and feeds on the
leaves of plants.
When it is still,
it looks just like
a twig.

The **chameleon** can
change its colour
very quickly so it
will not be seen. Its
tail helps it to hold
on to the branches
and stay still. Then
it shoots out its
long sticky tongue
to catch insects.

There are many strange creatures in the sea. The **dragonfish** protects itself by waving its long fins spiked with poison.

The **copperband butterfly fish** lives in the sunny waters of coral reefs. Enemies cannot tell which eye is the real one.

The **puffer fish** can swallow water and blow itself up into a spiky balloon. Then no creature can manage to eat it!

The **octopus** lives among rocks on the sea bed and catches its food with its eight powerful arms.

The **sting ray** uses its huge fins like wings to help it fly through the water. Can you see the poisonous spine on its tail?

The **angler fish** lives in very deep water. It has a light above its mouth. Smaller fish come close to look and the angler fish gobbles them up.

Why do you think the **pinecone fish** was given that name? It is also known as the pineapple fish.

The silvery fish with lights along its belly is called a **hatchet fish.**

These animals are strange because they can fly even though they have no wings.

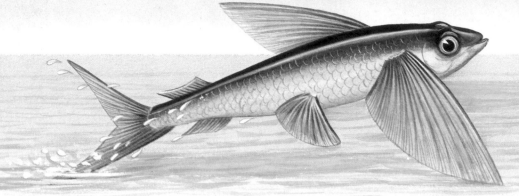

The **flying fish** swims so fast that it shoots out of the water. It uses its fins like wings and flips its tail.
It glides in the air
above the sea.

Adult **salmon** go back
to the river where
they hatched. They can
leap up high waterfalls.
At the head of the
river where they were
born, they lay their
eggs and then die.

The **sugar glider** feeds on the flowers of trees in Australia. It has flaps of skin between its front and back legs. These act as a kind of parachute and help it to glide from tree to tree. The female can even glide with a baby in her pouch.

Flying frogs have webs of skin between their long toes. They spread these wide and glide from one tree to another. They have sticky pads on their toes. These help the frog to hold on when it lands.

Many animals have surprising eating habits.

Snakes can stretch their jaws open very wide. The African **egg-eating snake** swallows an egg whole. Bones inside its neck crush the shell. The snake spits out the shell and swallows what is inside.

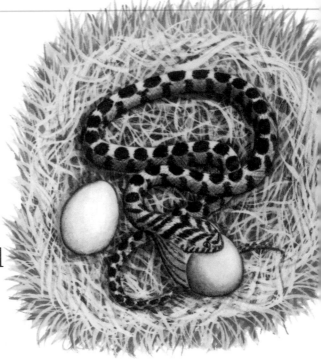

The huge **blue whale** is the largest living animal. It can grow to a length of 30 metres (90 feet) and weigh as much as 30 elephants. But it eats tiny sea creatures called krill. Think how much krill such a large animal must eat.

These animals use tools to help them feed.

The **chimpanzee** pulls the leaves off a small branch to make a stick. It pushes the stick into an ants' nest. Then it pulls it out and eats the ants that cover the stick.

The **sea otter** feeds on fish, crabs and shellfish. It cleverly uses a stone as a tool. It floats on its back and holds a flat stone on its chest. It bangs shells on it until it has cracked them open. Then the otter can eat the soft flesh inside.

Some animals make their homes in strange ways.

Bats hang by their feet with their wings folded up. In the daytime, and in winter, they hide in dark places like caves and attics. These are **horseshoe bats**. Can you see the shape of their noses?

The **water spider** lives in the water but needs air. It carries small bubbles on its hairy body and builds a big bubble under water held in a web. Then it lives in the bubble.

The **beaver** cuts down trees to build
its home on the river. It gnaws at
the trunk until the tree falls down.
Then it gnaws the tree into small logs.

The beaver's home is called a lodge.
It is made of logs, sticks and mud.
It has a hole in the roof to let in air.

The beaver also builds
a dam across the river.
This forms a lake
where the beaver stores
branches as its
food for the winter.

Some animals use others to help them in strange ways.

Look where the
elf owl is perched.
A woodpecker made the
hole in the cactus.
Then the elf owl moved
in with his mate to
make a nest.

The female European
cuckoo lays her eggs
in another bird's nest.
When the owner returns,
it sits on all the
eggs until they hatch.
The young cuckoo is
often bigger than
the other birds and
pushes them out of the
nest. The owner goes
on feeding it until
it is fully grown.

The **remora** has a suction pad on its head.
This sticks firmly to a big shark.
Remoras feed on scraps of food left over
by the shark, and they help to keep its
skin clean. They also get a free ride!

The Egyptian **Nile crocodile** has its mouth
wide open to keep cool. The **plovers** are
picking scraps of meat from between
the crocodile's teeth.

Do you recognise these creatures?
What is strange about them?
There is a list of names at the bottom
of the page to help you.

armadillo
crocodile
dragonfish
fire salamander
horseshoe bats
leaf fish
opossum
sugar glider
thorny devil
water spider